To Edward on the occasion of your First Holy Communion and Confirmation

Love & Prayers,

Mary (Lovatt).

10.5.15.

This book is not an end in itself. It helps support a good cause: the activities of the El Almendro Association of Buenos Aires that provides assistance to children, adolescents, adults and families in need and at risk due to abandonment, all forms of addiction, violence and marginalisation. The author, illustrator and publisher have decided to donate part of the proceeds from the sale of this book to the association, having appreciated the extraordinary work that it does in the Argentine capital.

The El Almendro Association (www.elalmendro.org.ar), which was founded in 1992, is now directed by Father Gustavo Mascó, who wanted to share a few words with the readers of this book.

Our Friend Jorge: Published 2014 by The Incorporated Catholic Truth Society, 40-46 Harleyford Road, London SE11 5AY. Tel: 020 7640 0042; Fax: 020 7640 0046; www.cts-online.org.uk. Copyright © 2014 The Incorporated Catholic Truth Society in this English-language edition.

ISBN: 978 1 86082 911 6   CTS Code CH 55

Translated from the original Italian Edition, **Il Nostro Amico Jorge:** written by Jeanne Perego and illustrated by Giovanni Manna. ISBN 978-88-215-9049-8. Copyright © 2013 Tipress Deutschland GmbH.
Text © 2013, Jeanne Perego.
Illustrations © 2013, Giovanni Manna.

Our Friend Pope Francis

The amazing story of Jorge Bergoglio

Text by
JEANNE PEREGO

Illustrations by
GIOVANNI MANNA

Look for Jesus and Mary

We must see with eyes of our heart, only then will we see Jesus. We should not look at Jesus in the same way as we watch a film at the cinema or a series on television. Remember, our aim is not just to see Jesus, he is not just someone to look at, we must truly meet him.

Why must we look for Jesus? To meet him. And when we have met him we must say from the bottom of our heart: "We have met, now stay close to me and remain in my heart!"

Jorge M. Bergoglio

From the Homily of the Mass for Children 2011

I ask you for a great round of applause for the Virgin Mary.

With Mary beside us, let us remember a saying of St Therese of Lisieux: "Jesus is in the little children and for this reason we must look after them."

Let us prepare ourselves to meet the living Jesus in the Mass and let us say strongly that we believe that he is present and alive in the Blessed Sacrament. Repeat after me: "We believe that you are in the Blessed Sacrament!"

And don't forget to make sure that your priests teach you the Gospel.

Jorge M. Bergoglio

From the Homily of the Mass for Children 2012

Foreword

Once upon a time… is how all fairytales begin. This isn't a fairytale, but it is a story well worth telling.

Like all fairytales, this story has a hero. In this book - Our Friend Pope Francis - the hero's name is Jorge, but the real star is God. Let me explain.

Even though we cannot see Him and many times we are unaware of his presence, God is in all the good and beautiful things of life. But you must know how to find Him!

It was God who with great vision and immense love created the setting, brought together people, and illuminated every event so that the young boy named Jorgito would later become Father Jorge, then Monsignor Jorge and Cardinal Bergoglio, and now Pope Francis.

However, our Holy Father Pope Francis was not 'invented' on March 13th. If we now see a Pope with the heart of a father, this is due to the fact that in the past he was a loving son and grandson, a good student, a priest who deeply understood his brothers in faith and a bishop with an understanding and great love for all the members of his family, the Church. In this great family, Pope Francis has always sought to help and continues to help people in need and those who are suffering.

God is the star of this story because he filled Jorgito's heart with his love. Jorgito is the co-star because he accepted the love of God, who has always accompanied and guided him, even now since he has become "Our Friend Jorge", the friend of God.
You see, in this story we are about to read, there are not just readers or spectators.

Reading about that young boy named Jorgito, we can all learn to accept God's love and to love others. That way we can become what Jorge is today: God's smile for the whole world.

           Mons. Eduardo Horacio García
           Auxiliary Bishop of Buenos Aires

Prologue

A puff of smoke.
"It's white!"
"No, it's grey!"
"It looks white to me!"
Another puff of smoke.
"White, white!"
"White! White! We have a Pope!"
"Hurrah for the Pope!"

On 13th March 2013 at 7:06 p.m., the smoke from the chimney of the Sistine Chapel announced the election of the man who would continue the work of Pope Benedict.

"We have a Pope! Hurrah for the Pope!" What joy! Not only in Saint Peter's Square, but in every corner of the earth where the message of Jesus is heard.

There was a great celebration in my main square Plaza de Mayo. But I - the city of Buenos Aires - could never have imagined the reaction when they announced from the balcony of that square halfway around the world that the new Pope was our friend Jorge. When that fancy Latin phrase used in these situations that starts with Annuntio vobis gaudium magnum ended with *Georgius Marius, Sanctae Romanae Ecclesiae Cardinalem Bergoglio,* the hearts of everyone in Buenos Aires started beating wildly - boom, boom, boom! - as only happens for the strongest emotions.

For a moment, all my contradictions disappeared - luxurious villas just a short distance from shacks with no water or electricity; expensive cars speeding past rubbish-filled carts pulled by the *cartoneros,* the people who collect rubbish in the hope of earning a few pennies; and children in elegant school uniforms observing other children forced to beg on the streets - and I became the happiest city in the world. Our friend Jorge had become the spiritual leader of all Catholics and he chose the name Francesco - Francis - to underline how the Pope would serve the poor and the people of the most humble origins with simplicity, just like the Saint from Assisi.

It was then that I thought it would be nice to tell you his story so you could get to know him as well as I do. That's why I asked for help from the squares, houses, lamp posts and chapels that are my friends, who know many things and want to tell us about him. Soon you'll meet the lighthouse with a very long memory, a house with 'delicious' recollections, a chapel that looks like a garage, and a lamp post that is a bit nosy. Listen to what they have to say. I'm sure that by the end of their stories, Jorge will become a good friend of yours, too!

The Argentine Yacht Club lighthouse

I've seen many, many people arrive full of luggage, nostalgia and hope. I welcomed them all: people from Italy, Spain, France, Russia, Poland, Switzerland, Britain, Hungary… and I wished all of them well: men and women, grandparents, children like you, babies, people who became successful and others whose saw their dreams shattered and returned to their native lands. I have been here since 1915, the first to greet everyone arriving in our country. I am the Argentine Yacht Club lighthouse in Buenos Aires, and I know all the stories of the immigrants who braved the ocean to come here. That's why I wanted to meet you and tell you what I remember, so you will understand how this story began.

I heard all these people talking when they disembarked from the steamship after difficult, boring trips that seemed neverending. They spoke about their bitter past and their fears during the crossing. Some suffered from sea sickness and others became ill. They shared their dreams about the future and they promised to meet again once they were settled, after they had made their fortune in this faraway country. I saw them hesitantly enter the *Hotel de Inmigrantes*, where they would wait until they had found their place in this world that was once just a word to them: Argentina. I saw and heard everyone who arrived from every part of the world beyond the stretch of water over which I stand.

Yes, I remember them well. I'm a lighthouse with a very good memory! It was 15th February 1929 when Rosa and Giovanni with their son Mario disembarked from the Giulio Cesare ship. Bergoglio was the family's surname. Even though it was hot and humid that mid-summer day, Signora Rosa kept her coat on with a large fur collar. No, she didn't want to show off; she wasn't the type, even though she was a fine-looking woman.

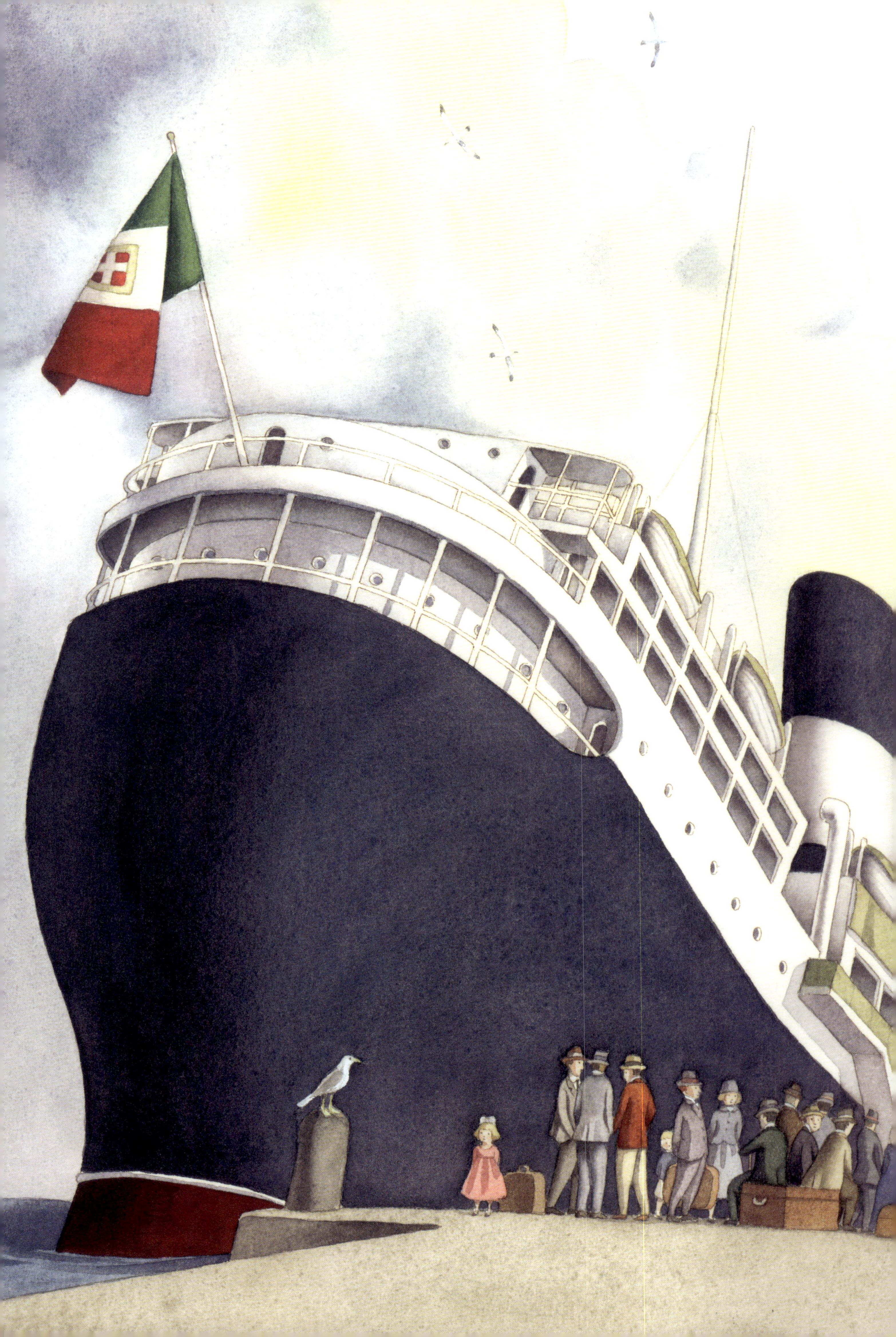

In the wide fox collar that made her sweat and pricked the skin at the nape of her neck, she had hidden all the money from the sale of their house and confectioner's shop in Portacomaro, their home town in Italy which is not far from Turin. Everything they owned was in there, stitched inside that collar, and it was going to let them begin a new life. It was a sort of furry safe!

While most of the passengers arriving with them went to the *Hotel de inmigrantes*, where they slept in dormitory rooms with 250 beds and where the women tended the children while the men went out looking for work, Rosa, Giovanni and Mario set off for Paraná, where Giovanni's three brothers moved many years earlier. *"Come join us,"* they wrote. *"We have a good life here and we could live close to one another and work together in our new business venture."* This prospect is why the young family bravely decided to leave everything behind in Italy and cross the ocean.

In Paraná, Giovanni and Mario immediately started working in the family business. They laid pavements and were so good at their jobs that they quickly saved enough money to build an apartment building for the whole Bergoglio family. There was one floor for each of the four brothers and their families and the building even had a lift, the first in the city.

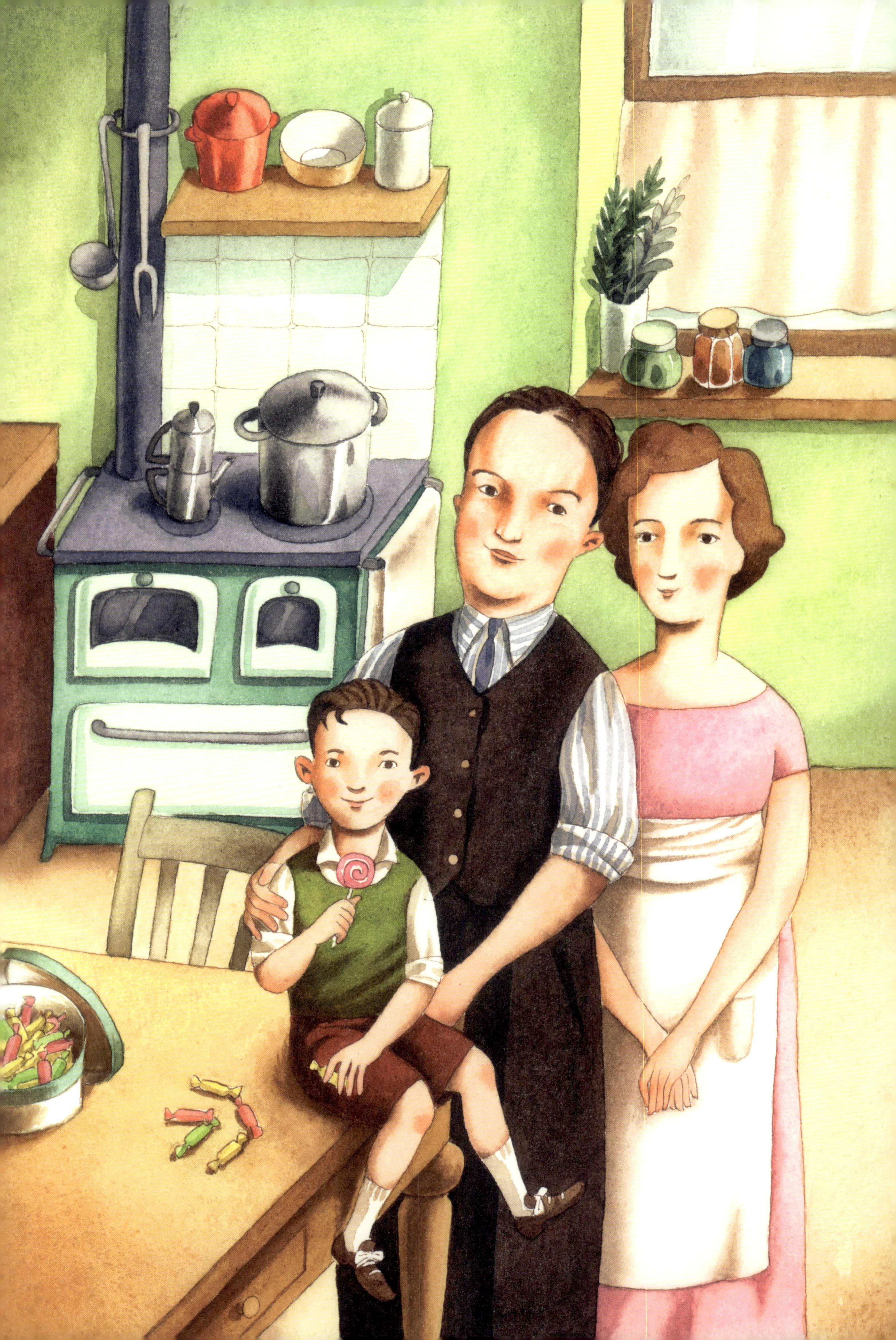

The house at 531 Membrillar Street

Welcome to the Flores neighbourhood! We've got so much to tell you about Jorge's life here, so let's begin. The 1930s were a dramatic time here in Argentina. The certainty of a good job and generous salary that convinced millions of people to cross the ocean vanished after the great depression. Nothing remained the same. Dreams were shattered and many people found themselves poor and hungry. Some people returned to their native country while others remained. Even the Bergoglio family business in Paraná fell on hard times, and the four brothers were forced to sell everything - even the apartment building with the lift - to survive.

Rosa, Giovanni and Mario packed their bags and moved to Buenos Aires to seek their fortune. Giovanni opened a grocer's shop and Mario, who was the bookkeeper for the family business in Paraná, helped stock the shelves and made deliveries to customers. Business went rather well and life was again serene for them here in our neighbourhood.

I know this because I am the house at 531 Membrillar Street where Mario came to live with Regina, his lovely bride, and their first child named Jorge Mario, who was born nearby on 17th December 1936. After Jorgito's birth, Mario wanted a bigger home for his new son and his future siblings.

To tell the truth, I wasn't all that spacious because even though I have two storeys now and overlook many low-lying buildings around me, back then I was a one-storey house like many in the neighbourhood. It was rather cramped for a family with five children, because Alberto, Oscar, Marta, and Maria Elena were born after Jorge. Anyone who came to visit back then saw that I had a living room, kitchen and bathroom.

The parents had a bedroom, the three boys slept in the other bedroom, and the two girls had to sleep on chair beds in the living room. But even though there wasn't much room, everyone got along and the mood was serene. I may not have had much furniture, but I was filled with hugs, kisses, laughter and happiness. The children were also raised with strict rules, which is how it should be in every family. Don't you agree?

Although the Bergoglios were not wealthy, they had everything they needed. Mario, who in the meantime was hired as a bookkeeper at a shoe factory nearby, could even splash out on food. Just think: he didn't want to see the same food served twice in a row! Therefore, if Regina, who was an excellent cook, prepared Milanese-style pork chops for lunch, she had to transform those leftovers into Neapolitan-style pork chops with tomatoes and cheese for dinner. I recall the delicious smells of her dishes: roast chicken with potatoes for Sunday dinner, pasta with braised meat sauce… Have you ever seen a house practically drooling at the thought? Well, that's me when I remember all those wonderful meals over the years.

It seems like yesterday when I think of those evenings at home, when Mario returned from work and gathered his children to recite the rosary. I never forgot the marvellous music that was played in my rooms. I can still hear the beautiful, irresistible notes of operas and tangos from the gramophone and radio that floated out of the windows to the small square where my Italians also played football.

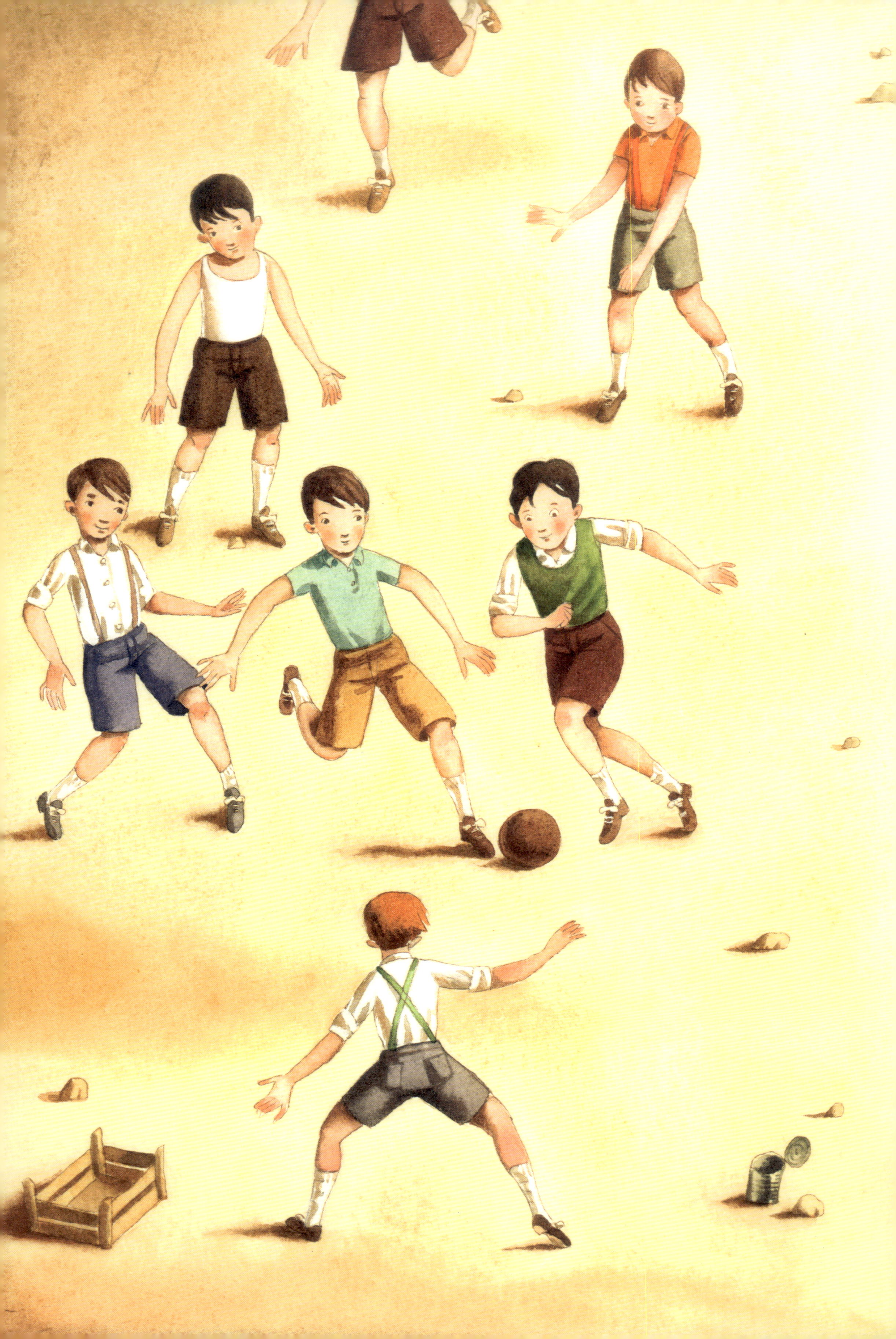

Herminia Brumana Square

Have a seat on that bench over there: now it's my turn to tell you something, and it's not just about all those exciting football games. *"Go, go, go!" "Over here!" "C'mon! Kick the ball!" "Goal!"* I remember those games very well. Everyone played happily together; if you wanted to have fun with friends from around the world, you could play football on this field. I was not the square you see today with my name on an elegant sign: Plazoleta Herminia Brumana. Back then, I was just a wide stretch of open ground that was ideal for running around and kicking a ball without having an adult start yelling, *"Get out of here or you'll break something!"*

Little girls skipped, played tag or hopscotch with a grid scratched in the dirt with a branch, while boys played endless games of football until the sun set. The only pause was for snack time with milk, bread and jam.

I remember all the children in those games: the *tanos*, which was what they called the children of Italian immigrants, the Argentineans, Spanish, Swiss and Germans. There was Rafael, Umberto, Osvaldo, Ernesto, Oscar, and especially quiet Jorge, who was so serious when he played. He never fell to the ground and faked a foul or ripped off his shirt when he scored a goal. Jorge was a fairly good football player and he was an enthusiastic teammate because he liked spending time with the other children from the neighbourhood.

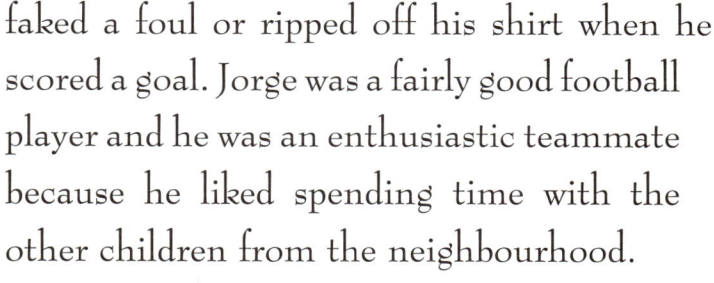

Sometimes he was a little too enthusiastic: one afternoon, he missed the goal posts and kicked the ball straight into the window of a home on Calle Membrillar! The glass shattered and apologies were made to the lady of the house who was not all that angry due to Jorge's politeness. *"I'm very, very sorry! We won't play here anymore. Can I help clean up the glass?"*
Jorge and his siblings were very polite because good manners were important in the Bergoglio home. His parents taught him to respect everyone and they raised their children without ever having to raise their voices. All they needed to do was to set good examples and throw a few stern looks when necessary. Mama Regina and Papa Mario were strict but also fun-loving. Standing to attention, they and their children solemnly sang the Italian and Argentinean anthems during national holidays, but they also joined the children in unforgettable water fights during Carnival. Carnival in *Barrio Flores* was so much fun back then! Everyone had a wonderful time together: parents from all over the world and children who grew up in one large family with the same problems and same hopes.

Thinking back, I remember little Jorge walking hand in hand with his grandmother Rosa when she took him to her home to help his mother Regina who was tending the other children. While they walked, Rosa would recite a few poems and prayers in the Piedmont dialect that she still spoke with grandfather Giovanni. Jorgito listened to her carefully and then repeated everything later.

I watched him every morning, even when he was accompanied to nursery in the school with the chapel where his First Communion took place. I saw him every day during primary school. Jorge cheerfully walked across me and I never once heard him complain. He never said, *"Do I have to go to school again?"* You could understand that he was happy to see his classmates and to learn something new, even if he certainly wasn't a bookworm. He learned maths by counting the steps going to and from school and, above all, he learned to read. Jorge loved to read! As the years passed, I would see him sitting on a wall or bench with a book in his hand. *"Come to play!"* his friends yelled during another football game, but he often said no. He wasn't in the mood. He would return to the pages of a book that had opened up a whole new world to him that few could imagine at the time.

The dome
of San José de Flores Basilica

I saw the Bergoglio family every Sunday. Mario and Regina arrived holding their youngest while the other children walked alongside them, holding hands. They climbed the stairs in front of the church door and went inside to find a place to sit during Mass. They were always well-behaved and smiling. During Mass, I saw those adorable *tanos* gaze in awe at the sparkling crowns of Saint Joseph and baby Jesus on the main altar and then at the painting above them of a little girl holding a lily in her hand. Perhaps someone had told them that this was a portrait of the artist's daughter who went to heaven after dying from a terrible disease. Other times the children looked at the painting in which the Virgin Mary watches Jesus and Saint Joseph carefully sawing a wooden plank in the carpenter's shop in Nazareth. Children who come here love seeing young Jesus hard at work. I know this because I'm the dome of the San José de Flores Basilica, and from high above I can see everyone who enters the church. Yes, protected by my tiles as black as slate, I'm in a privileged position to see and recognise people, to see what they are doing and to understand if they are happy, sad, or looking for help.

So sit back and listen carefully because what I am about to say is important if you really want to know Jorge's story. I remember seeing him when he was just a baby. I watched him grow and pay more attention to what was said in church.

When he was a young man, I saw him stop in front of the church after Mass with his friends and schoolmates from the institute for chemists and chat about football and basketball, about his favourite tango and milonga artists, and about funny situations like the parrot who lived next to the school and repeated everything it heard, even the national anthem sung by the students on official occasions. They used to laugh thinking of that chatty bird!

As he grew up, Jorge was like all the children his age, but there was something special within his soul. He realised that on the morning of 21st September 1953, when he and his classmates were going on an outing to celebrate *Students' Day*. That's what the young people do here: they welcome the warmer weather with a jaunt or a picnic in the park. On that day, however, Jorge did not show up at the station where his friends were waiting for him. While he was walking to meet them, he passed here and decided to enter to say a prayer. *"Just ten minutes and then I'll catch up with them,"* he thought. Mass was starting, and Jorge stayed for the entire service. Afterwards, he felt the need to go to confession, so he headed towards the confessional near the entrance: the one you see here next to the altar dedicated to the Madonna of Luján, the patroness of Argentina. The priest who entered the church with him listened to his confession.

After confession, Jorge sat in the shadows, his eyes gazing at Saint Joseph over the altar. He sat for a while and then he got up and headed home instead of going to the station. I could tell by his happy face that he had finally discovered his path in life.

Avenida Rivadavia

Hey! Can you hear me? It's very noisy here. Okay, I'll speak louder: you can't miss anything I want to tell you. First, let me tell you about myself. I'm like Thursday: always in the middle! If you want to go from one point of Buenos Aires to another, you have to come here to me. I'm the Avenida Rivadavia, the longest street of this huge city. I'm forty kilometres long - not bad, eh? Each day I see over eighty buses and a never-ending flow of cars that travel up and down from dawn to late at night. Then there are motorcycles, trucks, and vans; the traffic is unbelievable.

I watch everyone: people rushing to work and others who can't find a job, young people going to school and others forced to beg for money. I see people selling and buying things. I see the wealth of those who have everything and don't know what to do with it and the poverty of people who rummage through rubbish to make a meager living. I see people who have always lived here and others who came from afar in the hope of creating a better life for themselves and their children.

I've known Jorge since he was a child: he used to pass here with his parents to visit friends.

I remember him when he was going to the technical institute and later played basketball with his father at the old gas tower. I saw him pass by here when he was rushed to the hospital with a respiratory infection that forced doctors to remove part of a lung. Poor Jorge: how he suffered back then! Since then, he has had to take care of himself and avoid activities that require a strong body and resistance to the cold and physical strain. For example, he had to give up his dream of travelling to remote countries with difficult living conditions and hardships to spread Jesus's message of love.

I saw him carrying his suitcase when he entered the Villa Devoto seminary: he was so happy that day! His mother was not very pleased, however, and she needed much time to become used to the idea that her son was going to be a priest. When she realised that was what Jorge wanted, her heart filled with joy. Mothers are like that sometimes. Jorge used to visit her in the new home where the family moved when the house on Calle Membrillar became too small for them. On his visits, Jorge was always cheerful and ready to joke with his siblings. Over the years, however, he became much busier.

After he was ordained, on 13th December 1969, Jorge was sent to teach in other cities and even in Chile. His passion for studying encouraged him to enter the Jesuit Order, which primarily runs schools for young people. That's also why Jorge knows young people well and loves their company!

I often heard that Jorge was an excellent teacher, especially of literature. I'm not surprised: whenever I saw him, his nose was almost always buried in a book. He would read and read and read… sometimes even in Latin! But even with his nose buried in a book, he always noticed what was happening around him. And he realised that he could do something to change many things.

The Plaza de Mayo underground stop

He was always dressed the same way: black jacket and trousers, a black shirt with a white collar and a pair of very worn-out shoes due to the many kilometres they travelled. I always saw Jorge that way. And I saw him often because as the years passed, he became an increasingly important person here in Buenos Aires. He could have travelled by car and even in an elegant limousine with chauffeur, but he didn't. After studying a lot to learn all about Jesus and his love, Jorge became the bishop, archbishop and cardinal of Buenos Aires, and even though he could have conveniently travelled by car, he never did.

And when I say never, I mean never! He always used the train, bus and underground, especially the line that you take walking down my stairs here.

You see, I'm the Plaza de Mayo underground stop that is closest to the Archbishop's Palace where Jorge lived for many years.

Have a seat here on one of my steps; I've got many interesting things to say about our friend Jorge.

Carrying a black leather bag that showed its many years of honoured service, the man who never wanted to be called Monsignor Bergoglio or Cardinal Bergoglio, or Your Excellency or Your Eminence, but simply and only Father Bergoglio would discreetly enter the underground carriages. Sometimes people who didn't know him well would look surprised and even nudge one another, *"Hey! Did you see who that is? Bishop Bergoglio." "Cardinal Bergoglio? He's taking the underground too?"* During the trip, Jorge would recite the rosary or read: he wanted to be treated like an ordinary priest. But whenever anyone spoke to him, he listened carefully. *"Well then,"* he answered, *"Can I do something for you?"*... Once he even listened to the confession of a woman on a bus journey! She asked him unexpectedly and Jorge didn't refuse, even if the situation seemed a bit strange to him, too!

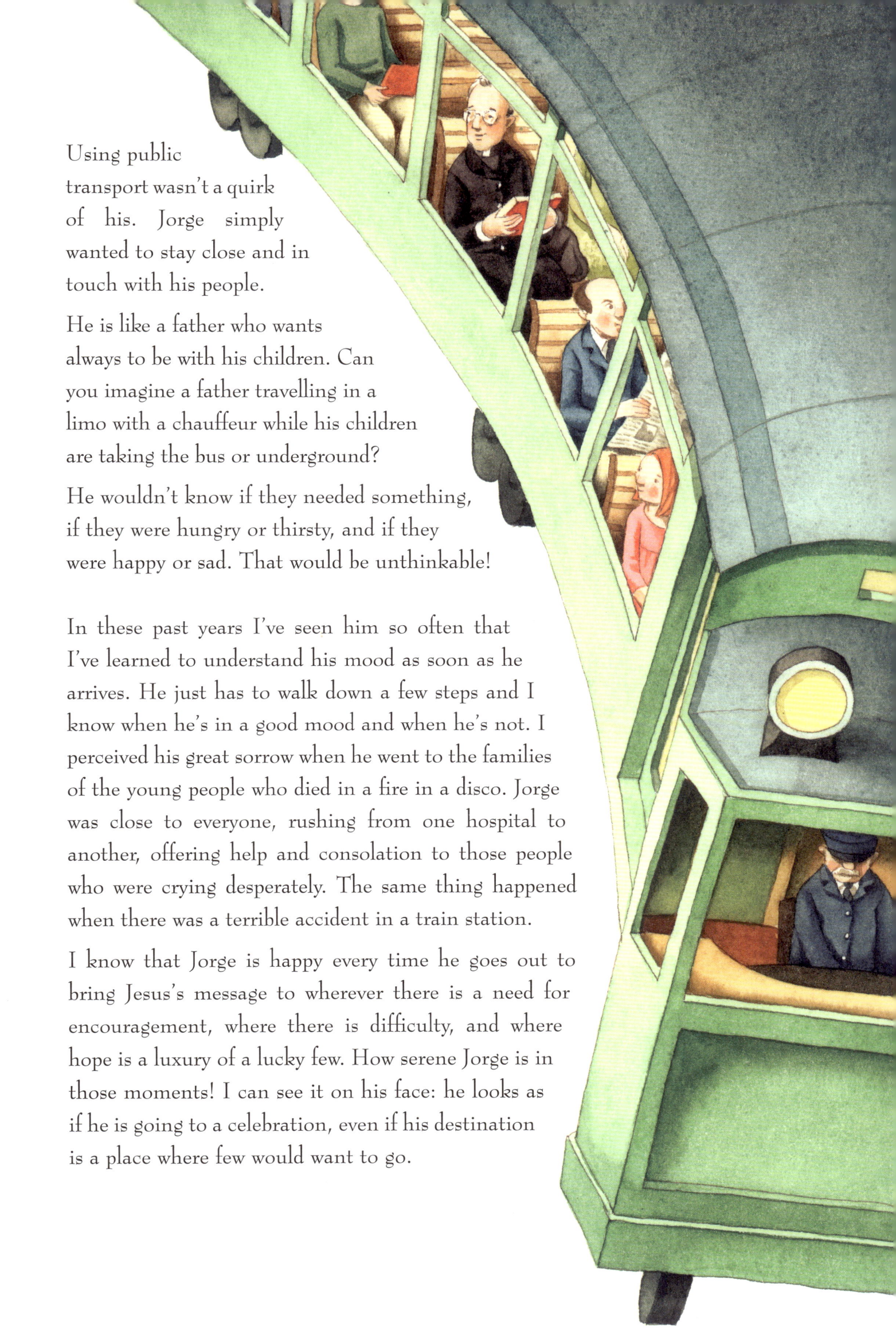

Using public transport wasn't a quirk of his. Jorge simply wanted to stay close and in touch with his people.

He is like a father who wants always to be with his children. Can you imagine a father travelling in a limo with a chauffeur while his children are taking the bus or underground?

He wouldn't know if they needed something, if they were hungry or thirsty, and if they were happy or sad. That would be unthinkable!

In these past years I've seen him so often that I've learned to understand his mood as soon as he arrives. He just has to walk down a few steps and I know when he's in a good mood and when he's not. I perceived his great sorrow when he went to the families of the young people who died in a fire in a disco. Jorge was close to everyone, rushing from one hospital to another, offering help and consolation to those people who were crying desperately. The same thing happened when there was a terrible accident in a train station.

I know that Jorge is happy every time he goes out to bring Jesus's message to wherever there is a need for encouragement, where there is difficulty, and where hope is a luxury of a lucky few. How serene Jorge is in those moments! I can see it on his face: he looks as if he is going to a celebration, even if his destination is a place where few would want to go.

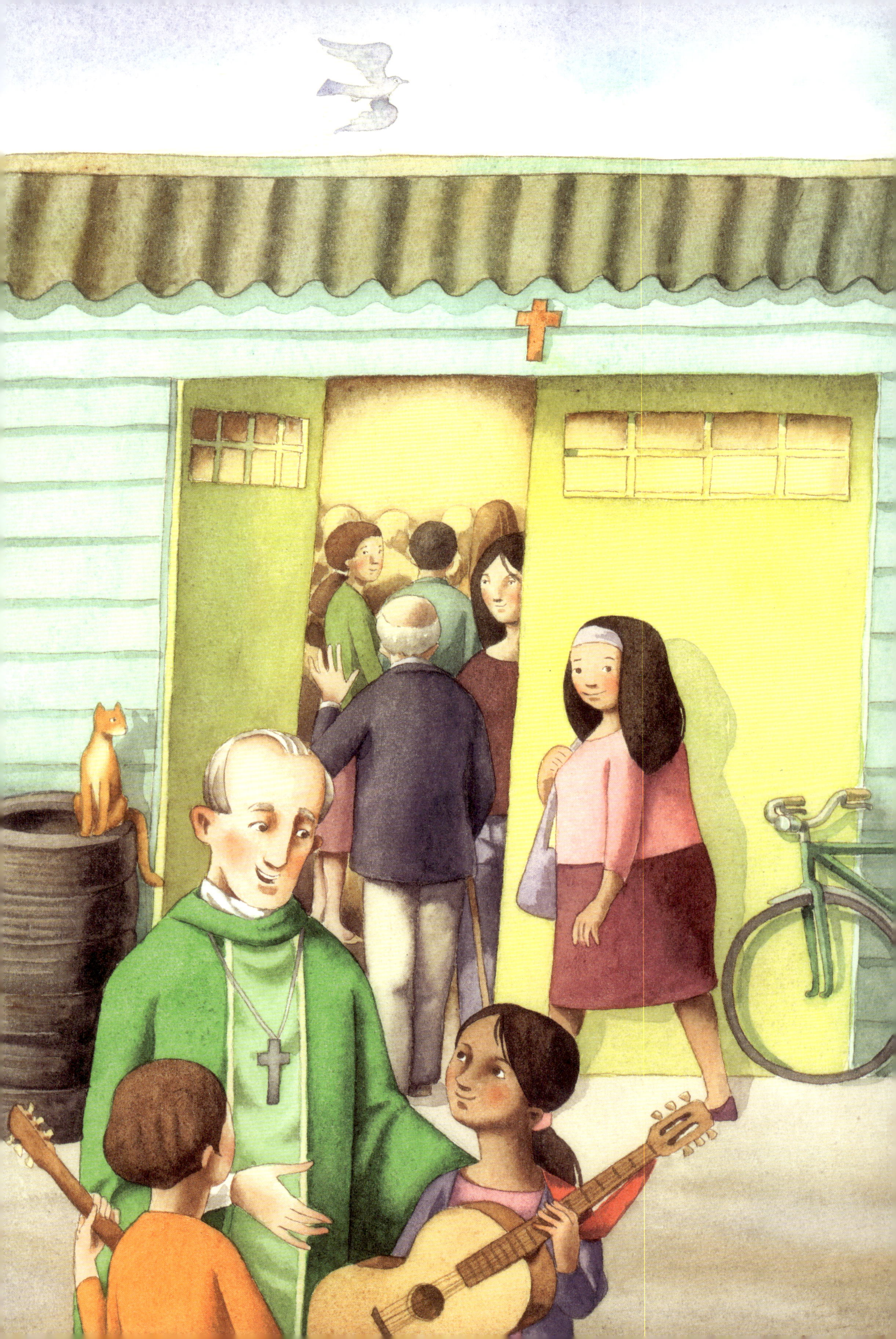

The Chapel of the Our Lady of Luján Missionary Centre

Yes, I know that I don't look like a chapel; I look like a big garage… or a warehouse. There's no trace of the gold and decorations of other churches. My wealth is different: it is the people who come here to meet Jesus. The strength of their love and desire to meet here to pray makes me a very rich church. So who cares about the fancy decorations!

I am the chapel of the Our Lady of Luján Missionary Centre, one of the parishes that Jorge established to offer God's loving embrace to those people who had no church in the neighbourhood.

So have a seat on one of our simple chairs; I've got so many things to tell you!

As you already know, the most important thing for our friend Jorge is meeting and helping others, especially people in need. Nothing else counts. I realised it immediately, the first time he came here. You understood that he was happy to have helped my community create a chapel where they could pray because before that, they only had a garage. Yes, you heard me - a garage! It belonged to two nice people who offered their parking space to the elderly and ill people in the area who couldn't reach the other church. You have no idea how many masses, baptisms, confirmations, and weddings were held in that garage! The car was outside and everyone was inside praying. Sometimes even Jorge came. In other places, a bishop or cardinal celebrating Mass in a garage would be shocking, but with Jorge, it would have been strange not finding him there.

As a matter of fact, it was normal for Jorge to go places that others did not. Here in Buenos Aires everyone knows that wherever there were people in need, you could be sure of finding Father Bergoglio, especially in the *villas,* the poorer areas of the city. Everyone ignores these places full of poverty and hunger and avoids going there if they don't have to. Here, many children live in the streets and no one cares for them. In these run-down areas, it seems that life has nothing good to offer its inhabitants.

Jorge used to go to the *villas* to say Mass, baptise and confirm children and to build simple chapels, or to visit priests who he sent there to work and help more unfortunate people. Always calm and determined, travelling by underground or bus, he would hold his black briefcase and he wasn't afraid of unpleasant encounters.

He was always ready to sit on one of the chairs in the mural-covered church that was once a garage to speak to people who wanted to tell him their troubles. If you only knew how many times he gave new hope of a better life to people who thought they had no chance whatsoever!

Jorge often found time to drink bitter *mate* tea and to eat a bite with a few of his parishioners, listening to what they had to say about their children's progress. He was delighted to know that they were well and going to school. Children always held a special place in Jorge's heart. If you want to know more, the best place to go is the stadium.

San Lorenzo de Almagro Stadium

Oh, there you are. Finally! Where do you want to sit to listen to what I have to tell you? How about the North Section where Jorge sat the last time he came to a game? Wait a minute, now I'll also start the fans' chants. That's it! The atmosphere is perfect: just like it is when the players are on the field.

Dale dale san Lore, dale dale san Lore
la hinchada quiere descontrol
da la vida por salir campeon,
dale dale matador...

Awesome, isn't it? Yes, our chants and songs are special: they're the envy of all our opponents! I'm the stadium of San Lorenzo de Almagro, the team that Jorge has cheered on since he was a child. He loves them! He even has a fan club badge in his desk drawer. Every week Jorge anxiously waits for the results, even if he can't be here in the stands and he watches the games on television. After each game he's thrilled or annoyed just like all the other fans, even if he's the first person to say that you also have to be a good sport about losing.

Jorge became a fan of our team because his father used to take him and the whole family to see the games in the old stadium. They were great fans and when they went home, Jorge and his siblings played in the square behind their home, trying to imitate what they saw in the stadium. *"C'mon, c'mon! Goal!!!!!!"* Jorge grew up but his passion for *Los Santos* remained. *Los Santos* is the name given to our players because a priest - Father Lorenzo Massa - founded the team. So since he was a priest, his players had to be... saints! Some people also call them *Los Cuervos*, which means "the ravens". Father Massa got the idea to form the team when he realised that the children in the Almagro district were at risk playing football in the street - one boy was even hit by a car. Therefore, he decided to welcome them to his church recreation centre. That's a great story, isn't it? Jorge was reminded of this when he saw Father Massa's statue in front of the door of our team's chapel. It's that modern building there near the entrance.

It was raining on the day that Jorge inaugurated the chapel, but he came anyway despite the downpour. It was the last time I saw him here, but I'm sure it wasn't the last time that he went to a stadium.

What? No! He didn't become a fan of another team: he'd never do that! I was referring to the stadium where he celebrates a great Mass every year in October for children your age who live in this city. More than 10,000 children sit in the stands and everything starts with a giant puppet show. Once there was Pinocchio and another time there were cartoon characters. It's really wonderful. And do you know who has the most fun of all? Jorge! That's because certain occasions bring out the child in him. Perhaps that's why he knows how to speak to children like yourself about the greatness of God's love and to console them when they have problems, as he did on Christmas Eve when he sat with a child in tears on the side of the road. People who were surprised to see a bishop sitting on the ground and speaking to a child certainly didn't know Jorge.

At the end of the Children's Mass, Father Bergoglio says goodbye - *ciao!* - just as a father would to his children. Then, by underground or bus, he returns to his office and prepares the right words for his next meeting, which could also be with one million people near a tree that is much like him.

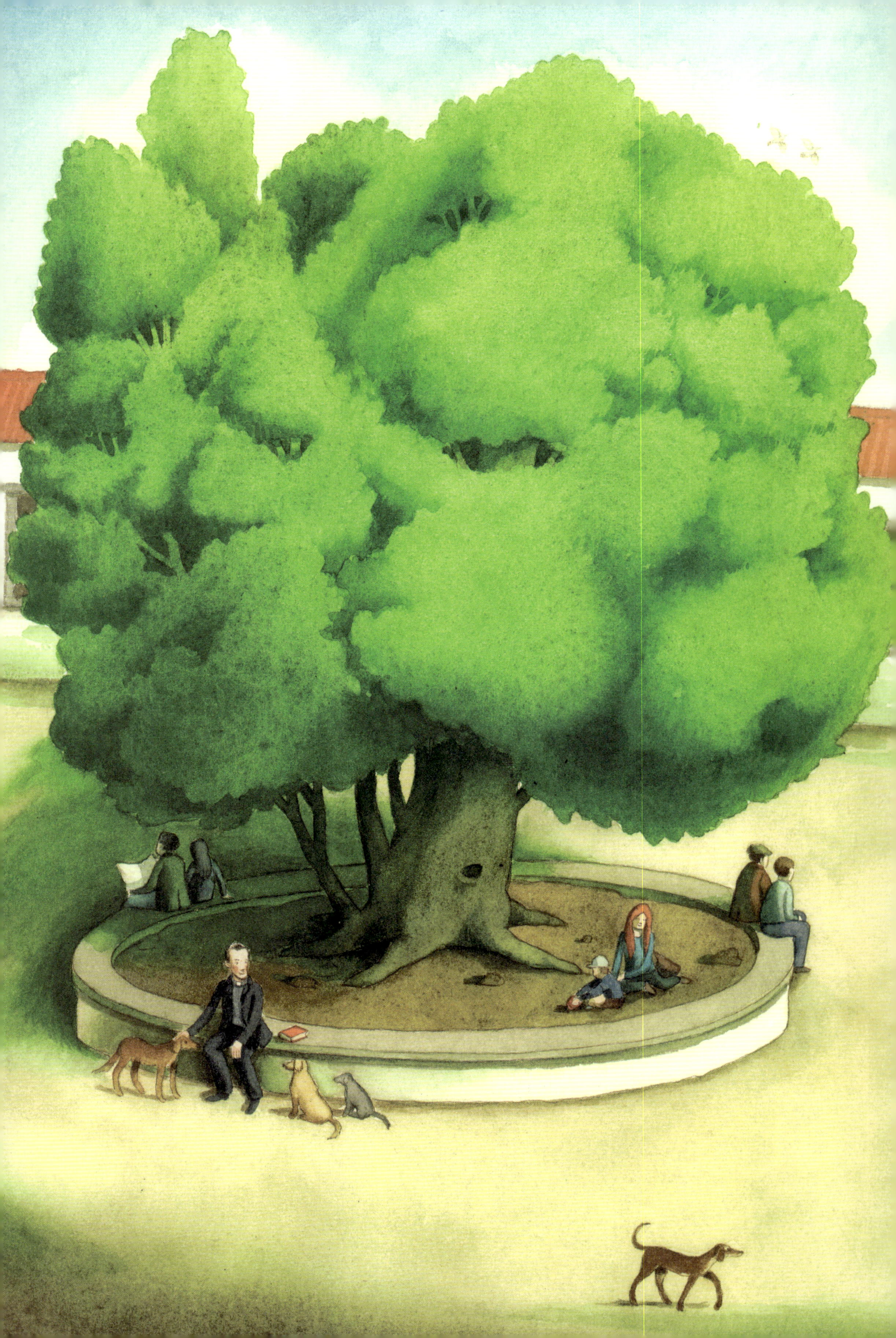

The ombu of Luján Sanctuary

According to a legend here in Argentina, when God created the world he asked the trees how they wanted to be. Some asked for a strong, sturdy trunk, others wanted a fancy crown as beautiful as a lovely girl, and so on. When the ombu's turn came, it said, *"I'd like to have many leaves to offer shade and shelter to people who must walk long distances. I don't want flowers or a scent or any flashy colours, juice or fruit. I only want to be of help to humans, to alleviate the weariness of the people forced to cross the plains, rivers, and mountains under the hot sun..."* Of course, the ombu was granted its wish. This is why the ombu is a large generous tree that is always willing to offer people in the Pampas and other parts of Argentina shade from the sun or shelter from the raindrops. I know this well because I'm the ombu of the Luján Sanctuary, the basilica where the faithful pray to the Virgin Mary to protect the people of Argentina, Uruguay and Paraguay. Every day the pilgrims who stop to admire the church find shade beneath my branches, and in the evening, my roots become the bed for stray dogs like Junior and Piqui who even go into the church and sneak right up to the main altar in search of tasty tidbits and a friendly scratch behind the ears.

At this point, you're probably wondering what this tree has to do with Jorge. There's a reason! We both have much in common: we're both strong, discreet, never flashy, and always willing to help others. I'm sure that if Jorge was a tree, he would be one of us!

I also had the pleasure of calmly observing him every time he came to Luján. Like every Argentinean, Jorge has always loved the Holy Virgin and I saw him kneeling in front of her statue many times. When he was alone, he arrived by bus and entered the church like an ordinary pilgrim. He would stand to one side and pray in silence, and then he would leave quietly. If he met someone who recognised him, he would smile and wave, just like an ordinary priest.

Jorge wasn't different during special occasions such as the young people's pilgrimage organised last October when a million people came to our basilica for High Mass during which they prayed to the Virgin Mary to protect our country. Just think: one million people! On that occasion, he arrived discreetly on Saturday afternoon, holding his briefcase and walking across the square. He wore the usual black suit. Then, while he waited for the young pilgrims, he helped the priests in the basilica confess the faithful until 11:00 p.m. He had dinner and rested for a few hours, and then at 2:00 a.m. he began confession again until the moment of the High Mass at 7:00 a.m. in front of the basilica, where his strong, resolute words touched the hearts of everyone there.

What's that? Was he tired at the end?

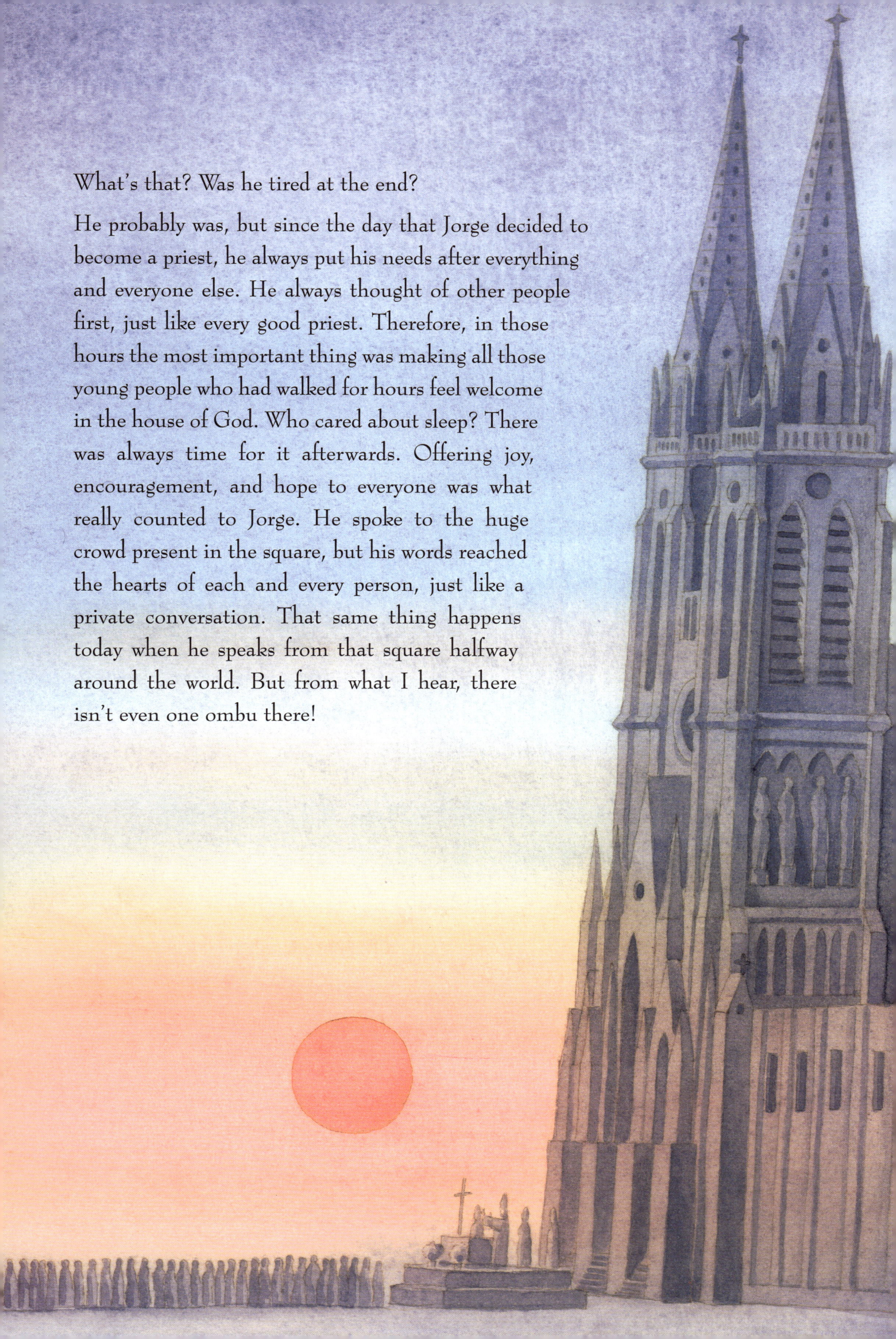

He probably was, but since the day that Jorge decided to become a priest, he always put his needs after everything and everyone else. He always thought of other people first, just like every good priest. Therefore, in those hours the most important thing was making all those young people who had walked for hours feel welcome in the house of God. Who cared about sleep? There was always time for it afterwards. Offering joy, encouragement, and hope to everyone was what really counted to Jorge. He spoke to the huge crowd present in the square, but his words reached the hearts of each and every person, just like a private conversation. That same thing happens today when he speaks from that square halfway around the world. But from what I hear, there isn't even one ombu there!

The Plaza de Mayo lamp post

Hey, over here! In front of the black iron gate with the silhouette of the Madonna of Luján. Look up! I'm the one who's talking to you: the lamp post of Plaza de Mayo, on the pavement in front of the Archbishop's Palace.

I've got so much to tell you about Jorge because we were neighbours for such a long time.

I used to see him when he would leave to go to his appointments and also when he was working in his office or relaxing at home. I could see him through the windowpanes. I know I'm nosey, but what would you do if you had to stand here all day long? Wouldn't you be a little curious, too?

Jorge's office was always very small with just a desk, a chair for himself and two chairs for the people who came to visit. That's all! He could have chosen one of the much larger and more elegant rooms for himself, but now you know our Jorge well, so I guess you're not surprised at the answer he gave when someone suggested it. He said, *"A larger office? Why? The one I have is fine, and I don't need anything more."*

In fact, his apartment on the second floor of the building was small, too. There was just enough space for sleeping and preparing meals, which were usually simple soups and salads, even though he was able to cook delicious dishes following his mother's recipes.

Jorge only wanted what was strictly necessary: just enough space for a few pieces of furniture and a few objects.

Jorge could see the square from his windows. I noticed the sorrow in his eyes each time he would look at the white handkerchiefs painted on the ground around the obelisk to commemorate the

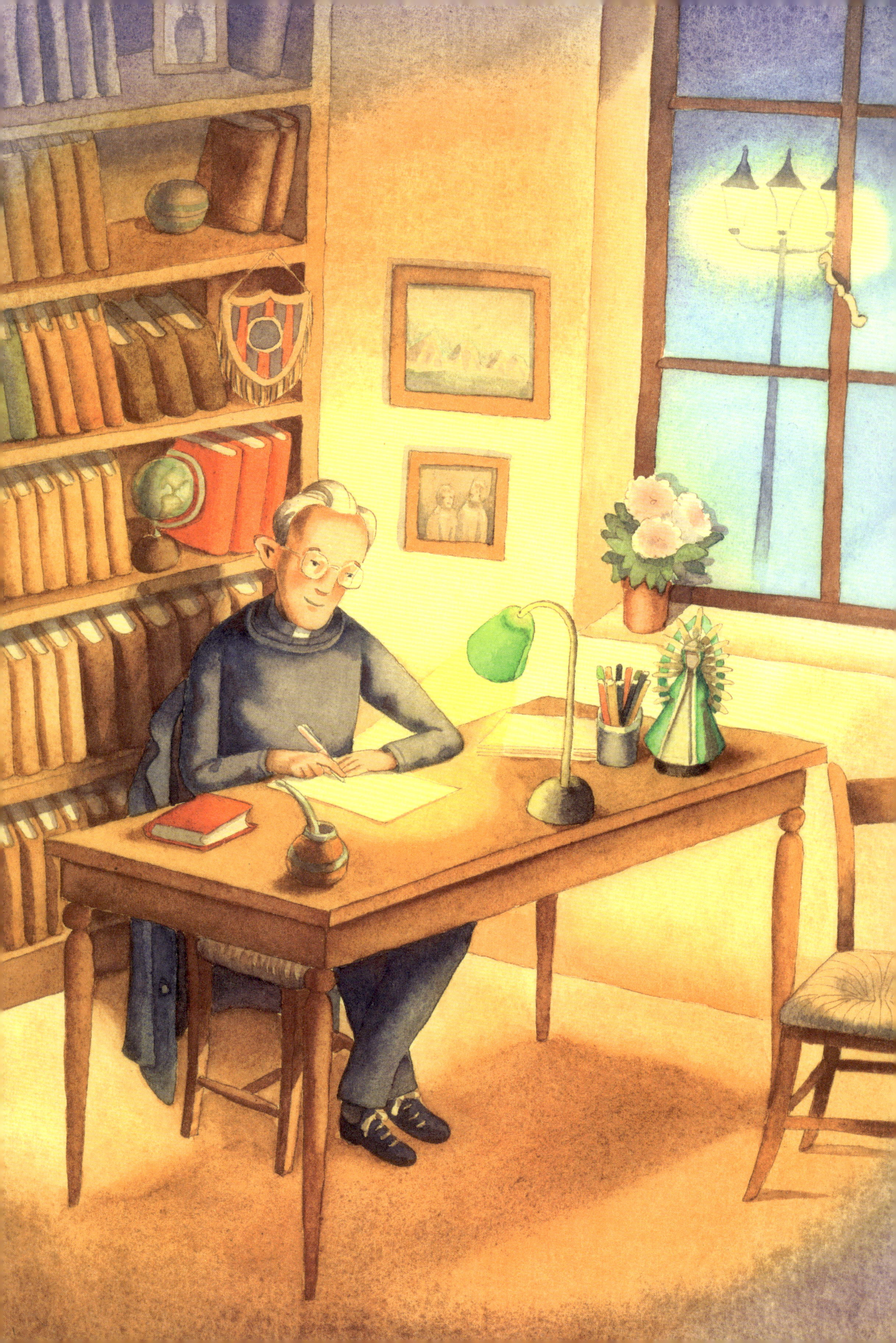

tragedy experienced by many mothers during the most terrible period of Argentine history. No one must ever forget the ferocity with which the regime disposed of thousands and thousands of people, who disappeared and were never seen again.

Everyone here knows Jorge and considers him a dear friend: the newsagent on the other side of the square who used to deliver Jorge's newspaper, the beggars who sit near the cathedral… To everyone he wasn't the archbishop or cardinal, but Father Bergoglio who always had a kind word and sometimes even a small gift for someone. Every year, during the solemn Corpus Christi procession, he would leave the head of the procession to greet the crowds, which totally ruined the organisers' plans. When Jorge was surrounded by people, you could always expect surprises!

The last time I saw Jorge, he was carrying a small suitcase with just a few things that were strictly necessary so he could spend a few days in Rome to elect the new Pope. I told him, in my own way, *"Have a safe trip and come back soon! We will be waiting for you here in the square."*

I was certain that Jorge would not have been gone for too long because I took a peek at his diary: it was full of appointments for the following weeks. Yes, I would see him soon.

But that didn't happen. A few evenings later, on one of the TV screens turned on nearby, Jorge himself appeared on the balcony of Saint Peter's to greet and bless the crowd. Our dear Father Jorge had become the spiritual guide of every Catholic! What a joy and emotion! If I weren't a lamp post firmly anchored to the ground, I would have started dancing!

Now I'm thrilled, even though I know that I won't see him crossing the square anymore to take the underground or to buy a newspaper, or to console a beggar in front of the cathedral. I'm happy because I know that Jorge is happy too, now that he can help even more people love life and have faith in the future. And that's what he has always wanted.

Our story ends here but it also marks the beginning of an even more beautiful one.

Afterword

Dear children,

This book tells the story of Pope Francis's life when he was a child.

Pope Francis and I met when we were already adults so, like you, I learned about his childhood through the stories told by his childhood home, the square where he played as a child, and the other places that shared their stories in the chapters of this book.

When Pope Francis was eight, he was much like the children that I help prepare for their First Holy Communion. Jorge was a good child, just like you: he read and studied, but he was also a good football player. He was always eager to learn, and this helped him prepare over the years and reach that moment in his life when he could share with others what he had learned. How I wish he were one of my students!

You can't imagine what I felt when, after that white puff of smoke from the Vatican chimney and that incomprehensible phrase in Latin, I saw Jorge Bergoglio appear on the balcony of Saint Peter's. The people standing next to me had to practically stop me from falling over because I almost fainted! I was so thrilled and happy! My pounding heart practically leaped out of my chest! My close friend, my honest and infallible advisor, the priest who dedicated his life to the most difficult problems and humblest people had been elected Pope. The entire city of Buenos Aires, all of Argentina and the whole world felt that same shiver of excitement.

Did you know that when Pope Francis was Father Bergoglio, he never abandoned me? He never forgot about me! He always accompanied and guided me in my home, when he was the bishop of Flores. He supported the idea of creating the "Nuestra Señora de Luján" missionary center in the Flores-Caballito district so that we could reach more people. He helped me make it solid and strong. It is the place where children and the elderly who had no church nearby to pray would join me and Father Jorge Bergoglio. They took Communion and prayed, and they were also helped: many families were given the opportunity to improve their working and living conditions and to allow their children to attend school. They felt that someone was helping them in life: and to think that our center used to be a garage owned by the very kind Roberti family! Afterwards, we built a chapel with the same altar from that garage and all the elements used during Mass.

Now that Jorge M. Bergoglio is our Pope, I still see him as I have always known him: he is true to himself and his actions always reflect his words. I see him as our guide. Francis was blessed: God saw in young Jorge the man who would have matured to wisely guide us with peace and joy.

Before saying goodbye, I would like to share with you some of Cardinal Bergoglio's words that accompanied and illuminated everyone who works to help children like you:

"It is extremely important to help children and the elderly: it is a priority. The hope of society lies in its children, who succeed us, and in the elderly, who share their wisdom with us." *(Interview in "Comunicarnos" issue 15 - August 2002)*

"We must enter God's heart and start to listen to the voice of the weak - these children and adolescents - and remember the Lord's words: "And whoever welcomes one such child in my name welcomes me." Matthew 18:5 *(Letter for childhood, 2005)*.

Father Gustavo Masco'
President of Asociación Civil El Almendro - Buenos Aires

Acknowledgements

It would have been impossible to write this book without the help of Claudio Marchiondelli, who helped me to discover Jorge Mario Bergoglio's Buenos Aires (and others besides!) with the eyes of an Italian/Argentinean. My thanks go to him for his patient help both before and after writing this text. A great vote of thanks goes to his family as well who put up with all the difficulties caused by his absence.

My particular thanks go to Fr Gustavo Masco for his help with contacts and documents. Many thanks also for the beautiful moments spent with his parish community.

Thanks also to those who spent time sharing their impressions, memories and stories, especially:

Maria Elena Bergoglio (I am grateful also for the recipe you shared with me!)
Mons. Luís Alberto Fernández
Mons. Eduardo Horacio Garcia
Fr José Daniel Blanchoud
Fr Ivan Dornelles
Fr Gabriel Marronetti
Oscar Lucchini

I also thank Anabella Barceló and Santiago H. Calvo who quickly resolved any final questions that came up.

Many thanks also to Marina Giacometti for her interest in the final phases of the work on this book and for the benefit of her knowledge regarding the Argentinean capital city: one couldn't have wished for a better guide to the most fascinating corners of the city.

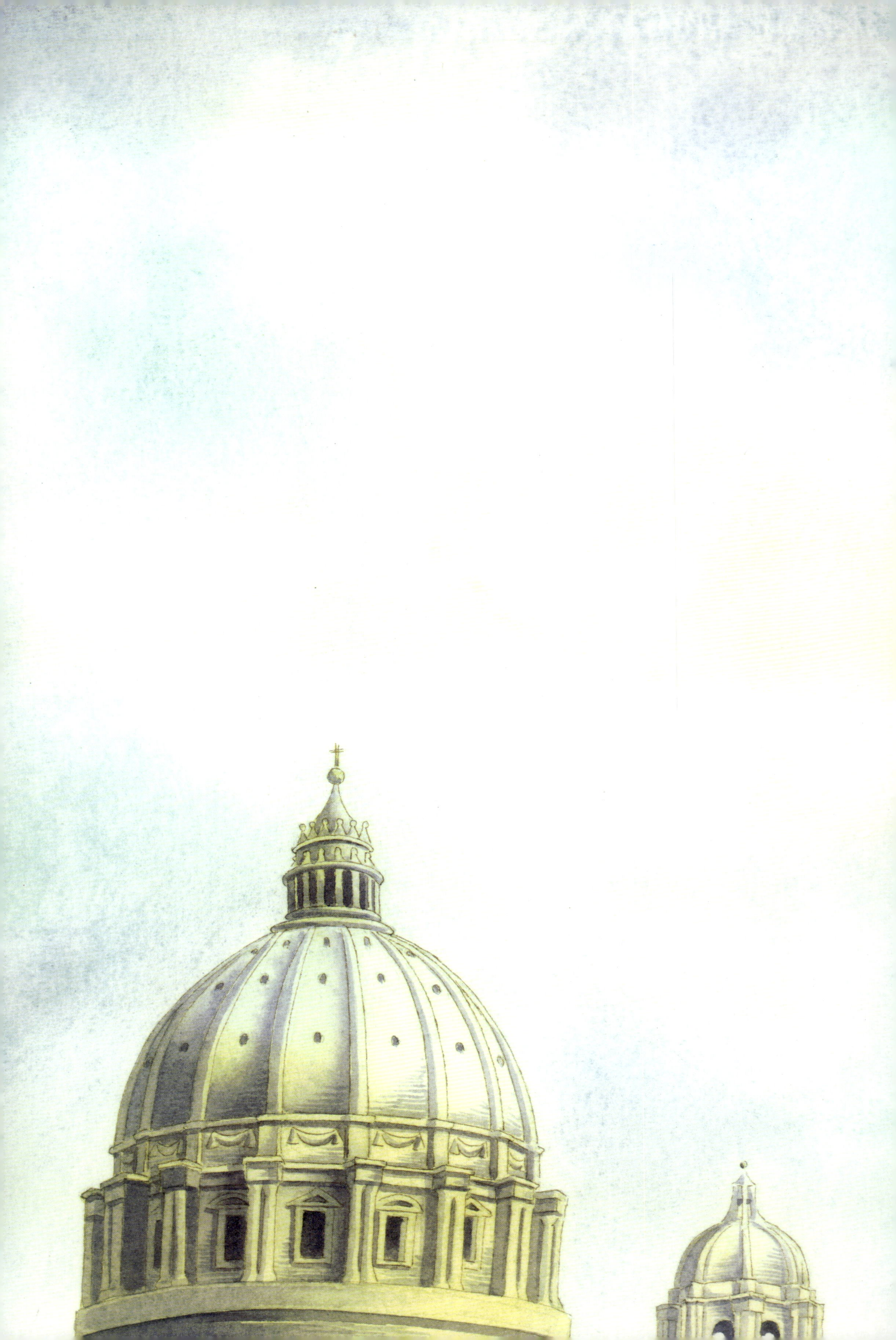